ACTION BASED OFFENSE

Framework for teaching offensive actions that create an advantage

Steven Kaspar

Action Based Offense by Steven Kaspar
Published by Steven Kaspar

4880 Normandy Ln
Memphis, TN 38117

https://stevenkaspar.com

me@stevenkaspar.com

What is Action Based Offense?

Action Base Offense (ABO) is a way of teaching and building an offense around smaller components or actions instead of traditional play calls

ABO gives you a way to call very specific actions that set your players up for success by putting them in the right position, creating an advantage, and capitalizing on that advantage as opposed to running fully scripted, continuous "plays"

The hope is that by breaking down offense into actions, both players and coaches will better understand the game and intention behind every movement - which is to gain and improve on an advantage. This gives coaches the pieces to make calls specific to all personnel - both offensive and defensive - on the floor

This is different from the traditional way of teaching offense where you have a play that has 4 or 5 different parts that are always run the same way and in the same order - and that normally flows back into itself

ABO is all about individual skill sets, spacing and floor positioning, making reads, and being intentional about every movement to create an advantage for your players to capitalize on. With ABO players don't worry about what's next in the play sequence or running it through - they are simply trying to score on the advantage created by the actions

Practical Example

There is a whole book here, but the concept is simple

Let's assume we are in a 5 out set with the ball on the wing

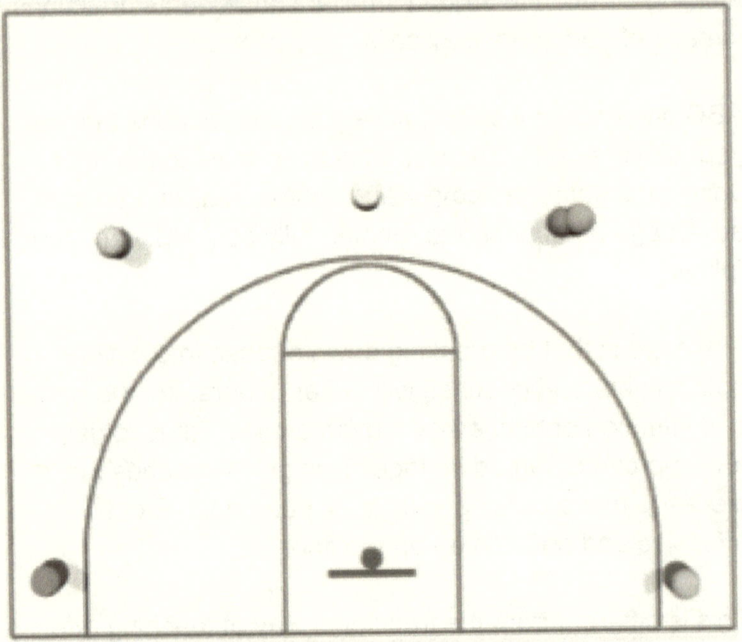

The call is "Swing Stagger"

"Swing" - swing the ball from one wing to the other
"Stagger" - set a stagger screen

You probably don't need it, but here it is drawn out

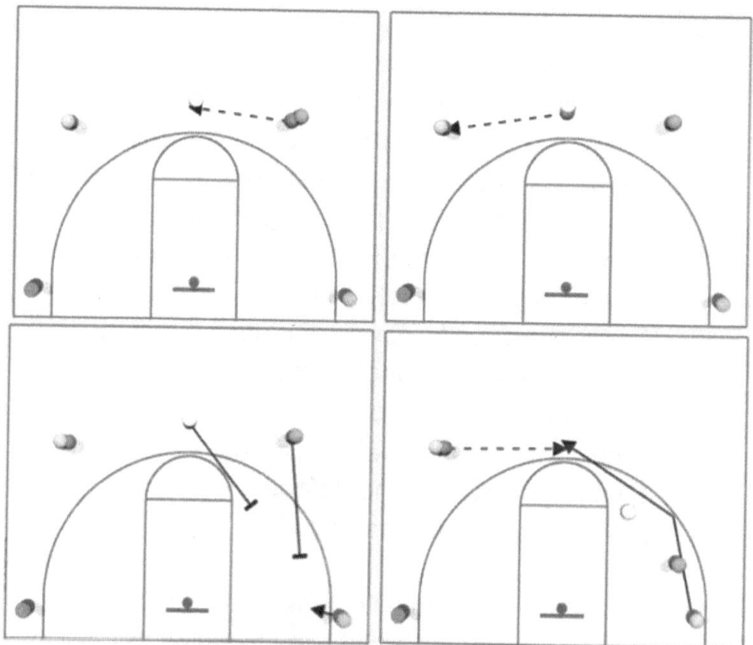

Offensively, our main goal is to create an advantage - meaning - we are trying to run offense that makes the defense either get out of ideal guarding position or they have to switch personnel creating a mismatch that gives you an advantage

Looking at the call - there are multiple reasons we might want to swing the ball first

1. Easier to get the ball into an operating area by passing rather than dribbling it down - maybe the defense is applying a lot of ball pressure on the point guard

2. We want a specific corner coming off the stagger screen - maybe one corner is a much better shooter or is good at curling and getting to the basket

3. We want a specific defender guarding the player receiving the stagger screen - maybe there is a very weak defender or a defender is in foul trouble
4. We want a specific passer making the pass - maybe your other wing has shown they are a better decision maker when reading a stagger screen
5. We want a specific defender guarding the passer - maybe they don't apply as much pressure
6. We want a specific screener setting the stagger screen - maybe it's your best player who you know the defense won't help off of
7. Simply swinging the ball can create a small advantage because the defense will need to shift slightly to adjust on the passes

And that's not an exhaustive list - there are all sorts of considerations for why we might want to swing the ball to the other side

Then we have the stagger - again, there are multiple reasons we might want to run a stagger screen
1. The defense isn't switching off-ball screens, so navigating a stagger screen will be tough
2. The defense is switching off-ball screens, so we know the player coming off the stagger will have a mismatch as well as the screeners who now have different defenders
3. The defense is playing very tight, so the stagger will get us in good position to attack the middle without much help because the help defender will be playing tight in the opposite corner and the other help defenders will be concerned with navigating the stagger screen

Again, the list could go on and it will be specific to every game's details

But this is where ABO really breaks from the traditional way of designing offense. We aren't running this stagger screen knowing if we don't score, we are getting to a stagger screen on the other side or that we will flow into a ball-screen

Why is that a big deal? That means all our players' mental resources are being used to figure out how to score on this stagger. They have complete freedom to make the best read because if they pop, instead of curl, it isn't going to mess up the rest of the play because there is no rest of the play

The stagger screen will give us an advantage some type of way
- If the defense runs under the screen, pop or fade for a 3
- If the defense runs over the top, curl to the basket
- If the defense switches, the guard can pop and now you have a big defender trying to keep up with your guard at the top of the key with the middle completely open or you have a guard on your big screener who can now post a smaller defender
- If the defense hedges the screen, the screener can slip to the basket or the guard can curl tight and get a layup
- The list could go on…

You might think that is overly simplistic, but the objective on offense is to create and improve on an advantage until you have an optimal-value shot. Many times - traditional offenses create an advantage and immediately lose it because players are so concerned with running the play

If you are still doubtful, I challenge you to go back and watch film, and see how often your plays get you an advantage that you improve on. I've seen a lot of offenses that do create great advantages, but players give back opportunity after opportunity because they are so concerned with running the offense through

Action Based Offense allows coaches and players to be on the same page and clearly communicate what they are trying to do - score the ball

Just in this book we will go through 20+ actions you can combine to make sure you are getting the right personnel where they need to be and coming off an action that will put them in a good position to make a play

Coaching Benefits

If you're a coach, I can almost guarantee one of your biggest struggles is getting your players to understand when to "run the offense" and when to "make a play". With ABO, there is a lot less running offense and a lot more making the play

ABO also gives a structured way to teach the game and a shared language to communicate with players. Teaching the game like this even helps when it comes to defense because your entire team will share the same vocabulary when describing the opponent's offense

ABO gives a framework for designing offense specific to each game situation. No more spending half a practice putting specific plays in for a game because ABO allows you to create "plays" on the fly. In my coaching, we had games where we ran a different combination of actions each time down the floor in a quarter, some of the call sequences we hadn't done in weeks, but since the team had been taught actions, they knew exactly what to do with different combinations

Player Benefits

Players love this because it gives them confidence knowing what they are trying to do offensively and that there is purpose with each movement

Players know that they can operate with freedom within the calls because there is no play they are going to mess up by taking what the defense gives them

Not Interested?

If you're not interested, email me at me@stevenkaspar.com with your venmo and I'll refund your purchase If you are interested, continue on

Teaching ABO

The great thing about actions is that they are simple and easy to learn. We have 20+ actions in this book, but you can start implementing ABO with a handful of them that you can teach with 15 minutes of practice time

A little learning theory before moving on...

When teaching these actions, it's helpful to understand 3 concepts of learning - Retrieval, Spacing, and Interleaving

Retrieval

Long-term learning happens when the learner is forced to retrieve a piece of information with as much difficulty as possible while still being successful. Don't give players all the answers. You feeding them the answer isn't going to produce long-term learning

Spacing

To create ideal retrieval difficulty, space the retrieval an appropriate amount. A learner needs to forget something from short-term memory for the retrieval to be effective and cause long-term learning. Teach a concept - move on to something else - then come back to the concept and have the players retrieve it on their own with as little help is possible

Interleaving

The more the learning environment is like the real-world demand - the better long-term results you will see. Practicing the same action over and over again might look like it's helping, but is that how you are going to call plays in a game? "Spread" - "Spread" - "Spread" - "Ok now,

Stagger" - "Stagger". No, you are going to call "Spread" - "Stagger" - "Pin-down".

When reviewing and practicing, interleave the different actions, so the retrieval is similar to what it's going to be like in a game. Once they have the actions down, put a defense on them

Ok, that's it on learning theory…

I would start with 1 set and 4 actions to get your team going. The *5-Out* set with *Swing*, *Spread*, *Stagger*, and *Away* actions will give you a lot to work with. These are covered in more detail later, but here is a quick breakdown

- *5-Out Set* - 2 Corners, 2 Wings, and 1 Trailer

- *Swing* - Wing has the ball. Wing passes it to Trailer. Trailer passes to the Weak-Side Wing

- *Stagger* - Wing has the ball. Weak-Side Wing and Trailer set a stagger screen for Weak-Side Corner

- *Spread* - Wing has the ball. Trailer sets a ball screen for Wing

- *Away* - Wing has the ball. Trailer sets a screen for Weak-Side Wing. If Weak-Side Wing curls to the basket, Trailer comes back for the pass from Wing and gets to a handoff. If Weak-Side Wing pops, Trailer can come back and set a ball screen for Wing who is now at the top of the key

Those 4 actions should be enough for you to get a feel for how ABO works, and they are a great starting place for seeing it in action

Day 1

After your warmup, put 5 players out in their new positions. For our *5-Out* set, we have 2 Wings, 2 Corners, and 1 Trailer who is at the top of the key

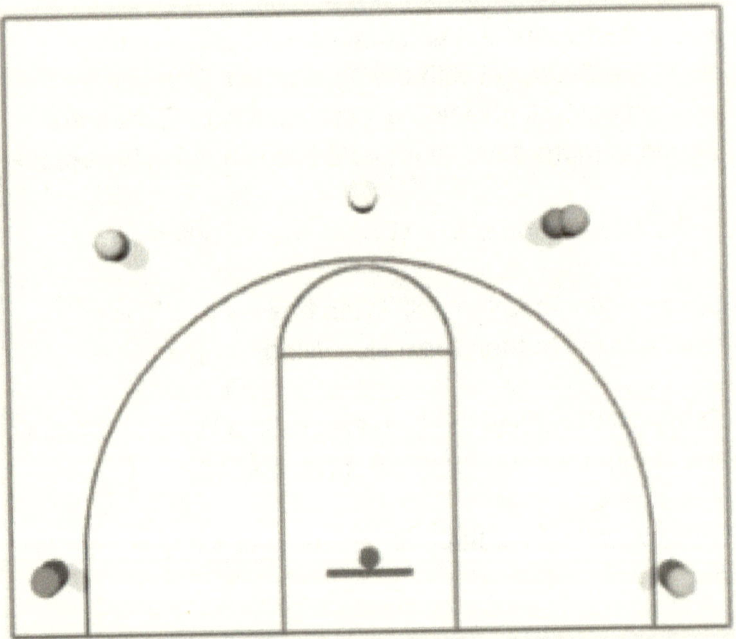

Ask your team if anyone knows what a Stagger screen is. (Now look at your best player and they will be giving you a blank stare - who are we expecting to have taught them this?) If they do know, have them explain it and then run through it scoring off a Stagger curl. Then, have the rest of your groups of 5 do it

> I would wait on having each player run it from every spot just yet

Then go through each of the 4 actions (Swing, Stagger, Spread, Away), doing the same thing. It should take around 5 minutes. Then move on to something else entirely letting them lose the actions from short-term memory

When you take your next water break, split the groups of 5 up on different ends starting at half-court, call out the actions, and have them run them

> Depending on how easy they got the first round - you may try having them change positions this time, but still don't have them run it from every position as it will get boring and not be very engaging

- "Spread"
- "Stagger"
- "Swing Stagger"
- "Away"
- "Swing Spread"
- "Swing Away"

This won't be game speed - they will struggle as they try to remember (retrieve) - let them struggle with as few hints as possible

Throughout the rest of practice, do this same process 1 or 2 more times before water breaks or during drill transitions mixing up the order of the calls

When it's time to scrimmage, tell them to call the actions and if they forget about one, call it for them, but let them figure it out on the floor. You'll be surprised at how comfortable they will get with different actions and enjoy selfishly thinking through calls to get themselves shots

Days 2-50

Days 2-50 Look the exact same as Day 1, but with more actions and more combinations. If you add 3 or 4 actions every two days, you will have 20 actions ready to go by your first game, and you can come down the floor calling "exchange swing stagger-pop pin-down" (this is an actual game combination we would call pretty often - with a different name). If you effectively interleave the actions as you add them, your players will have no problem learning 20 of them and being able to string them together

Actions

So now you hopefully understand the concept of ABO and how to introduce it to your team. Let's go through some actions you can introduce to your team

> *Please do research and watch games and add your own actions. It can also be helpful to teach an action you may never run because you will probably see another team run it at some point in your season, and if your team knows how to run it, they will be able to defend it better*

As a coach, I think it's helpful to think about the actions in subsets. Primarily, Movements, Passes, Off-ball Screens, and Ball Screens (and of course Other) (put these on a notecard for games, so you don't forget about one)

When describing actions below, I'm assuming the 5-Out set we have used so far (2 Wings, 2 Corners, 1 Trailer at the top of the key) and that the ball is starting on the wing

Movements

Movements move players around to either get better spacing or to get specific personnel in a different position to come off another action. For example, if your best scorer is in a Corner, but you want them involved in an action that starts from the wing, you can call Exchange to get your Corner to the wing

Exchange

Wing and Corner change places. This can be done with a handoff if Wing has the ball

"Exchange Weak" can also be called to create movement away from the ball

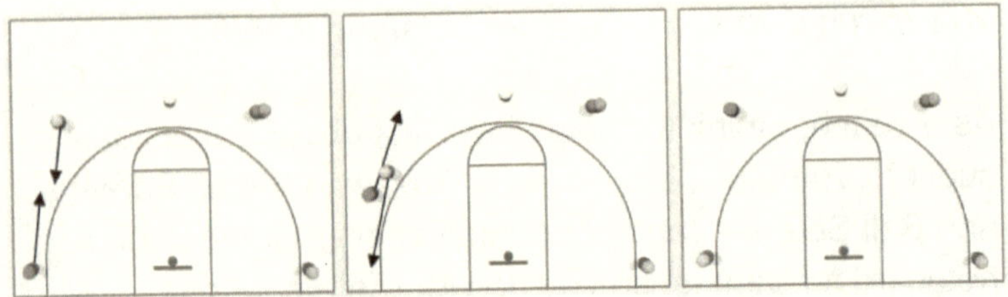

Examples: "Exchange Center Pin-Down", "Exchange Swing Stagger", "Center Pistol Exchange Weak"

Lift

Corner lifts to FT line extended

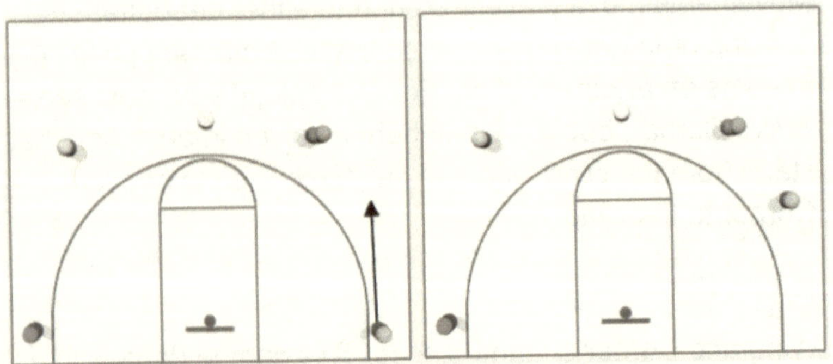

Examples: "Lift Corner Flare", "Lift Center Flare", Lift Corner Scissors Swing Spread"

Drop

Corner drops to block or dunker spot. "Drop weak" - Weak Corner goes to block or dunker spot

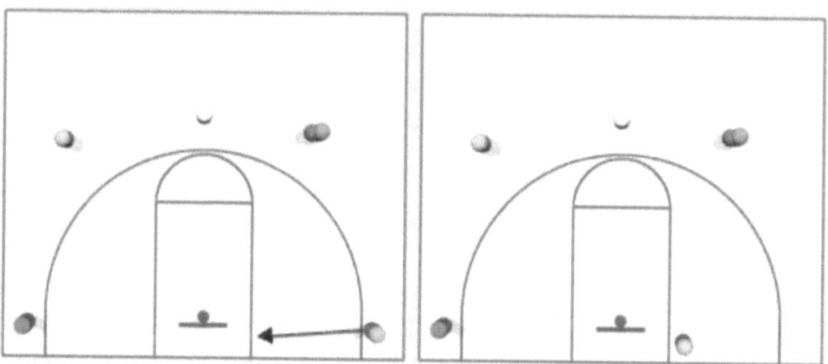

Examples: "Drop Swing Spread", "Drop Away"

Push

Corner pushes to opposite block or dunker spot. "Push weak" - Weak Corner goes to opposite block or dunker spot

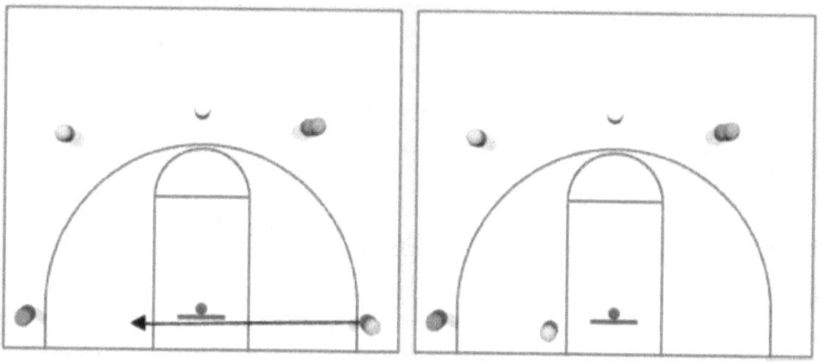

Examples: "Push Spread", "Push Flex", "Push Swing Double"

Swap

Both wings shallow cut at the free throw line to switch
spots

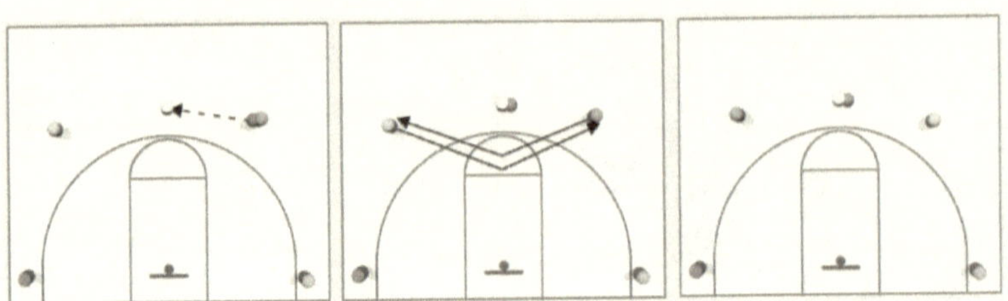

*Examples: "Center Swap Weak Double", "Center Swap
Stagger"*

Scissors

Both wings go over the top of Trailer, down the lane lines,
and out to the corners. Corners lift if they are not on the
wing already

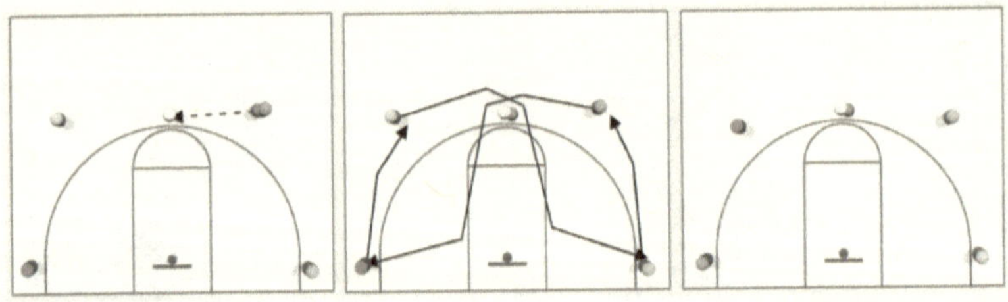

*Examples: "Center Scissors Pistol Weak", "Lift Corner
Scissors Spread"*

Passes

Swing

Pass the ball to Trailer and then to Weak-Side Wing

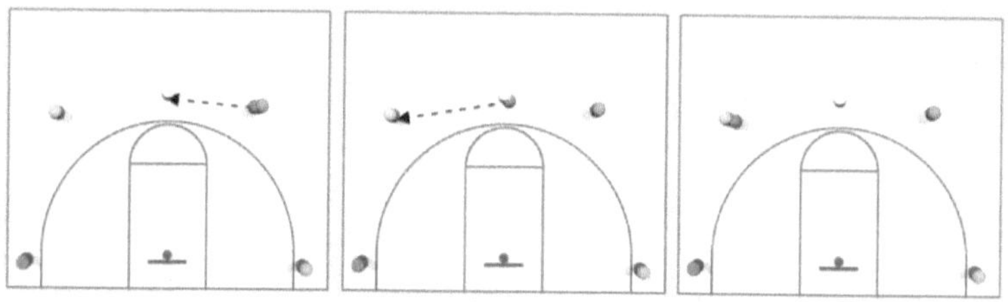

Examples: "Swing Spread", "Swing Stagger", "Exchange Swing Double"

Skip

Pass the ball from Wing to Weak-Side Wing (skipping Trailer)

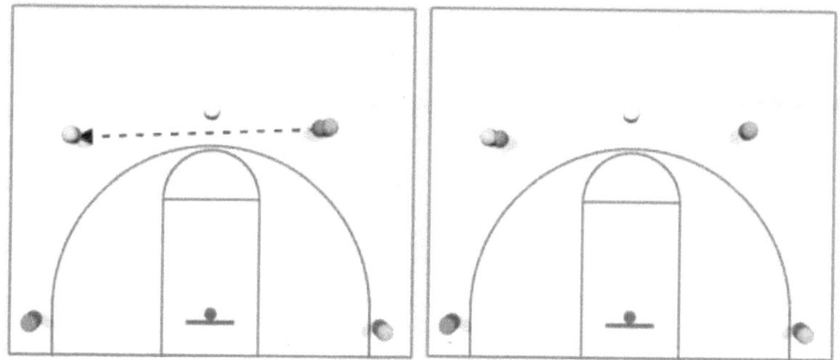

Examples: "Skip Stagger", "Skip Step-Up", "Exchange Skip Pinch"

Center

Pass the ball from Wing to Trailer

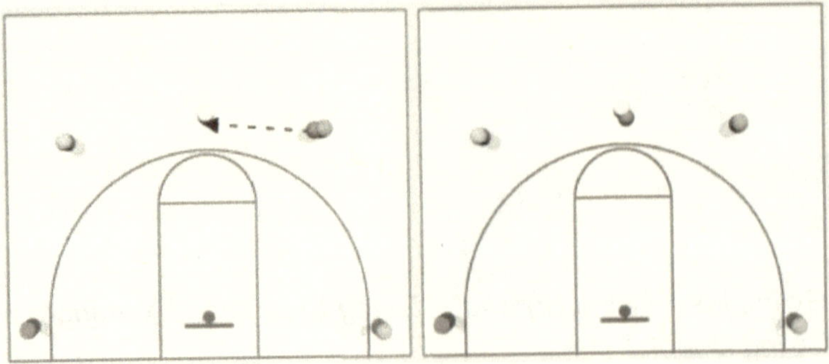

Examples: "Center Pin-Down", "Exchange Center Dribble-At Weak", "Center Swap Weak Pinch"

Corner

Pass the ball from Wing to Corner. We've used the same terminology for a wing to free-throw line extended pass. An example call would be, "Lift Corner"

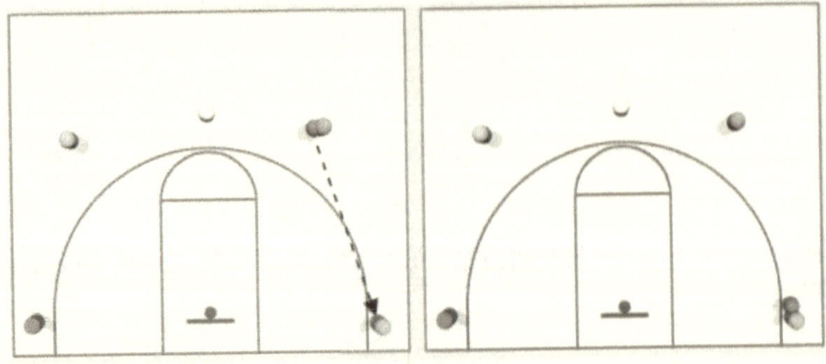

Examples: "Corner Away", "Corner Stagger", "Lift Corner Flare"

Ball Screens

Double

Weak-side Wing and Trailer set a double screen for Wing ball handler

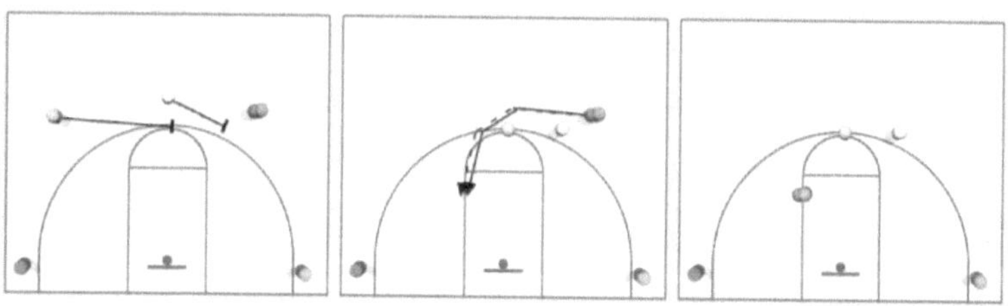

Examples: "Double", "Swing Double", "Exchange Swing Double"

Stack

Weak-Side Wing comes to the strong-side elbow. Trailer sets a ball screen for Wing. The Weak-Side Wing (now at the elbow) sets a back-screen for Trailer who just set the ball screen

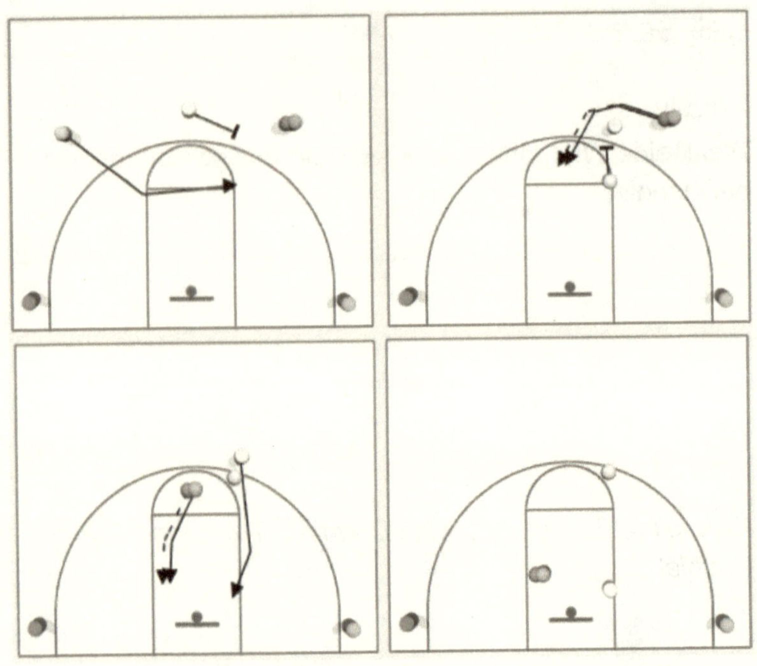

Examples: "Stack", "Swing Stack", "Exchange Stack"

Step-Up

Corner, low-block, or dunker spot steps up to set a ball screen for Wing

Examples: "Step-Up", "Swing Step-Up", "Swing Stagger Step-Up"

Ram

Trailer sets an off-ball screen for Weak-Side Wing who then sets a Spread ball screen for Wing. It can also be run by pushing Corner and then Trailer sets a Pin-Down screen for the player on the block who then comes up for the ball screen

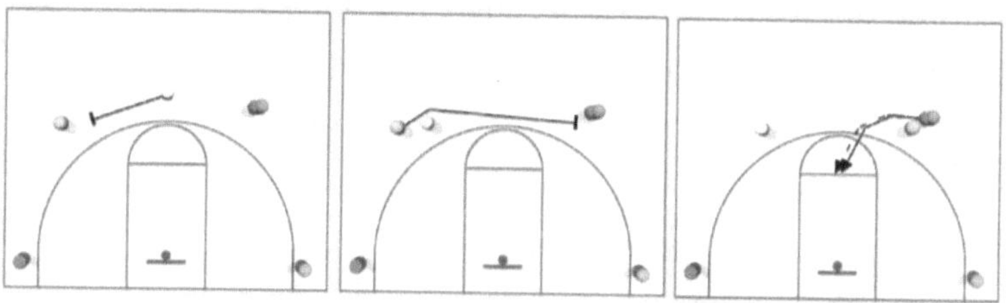

Examples: "Ram", "Drop Swing Ram", "Swing Ram"

Spread

Trailer sets a ball screen for Wing

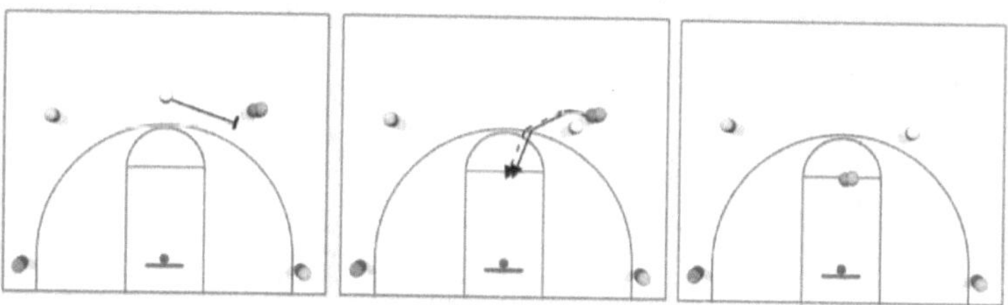

Examples: "Spread", "Swing Spread", "Exchange Swing Spread"

Pinch

Trailer and Corner set a ball screen for Wing from each angle. Trailer setting a Spread and Corner setting a Step-Up screen

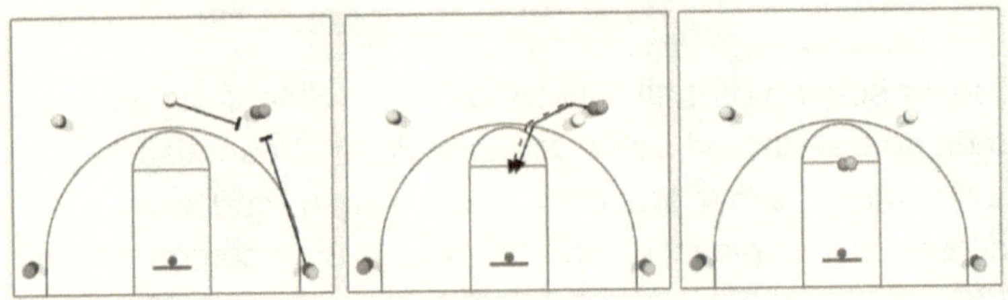

Examples: "Pinch", "Swing Pinch", "Center Pin-Down-Pop Pinch"

Off-Ball Screens

Stagger

Trailer and Weak-Side Wing set a stagger screen for Corner

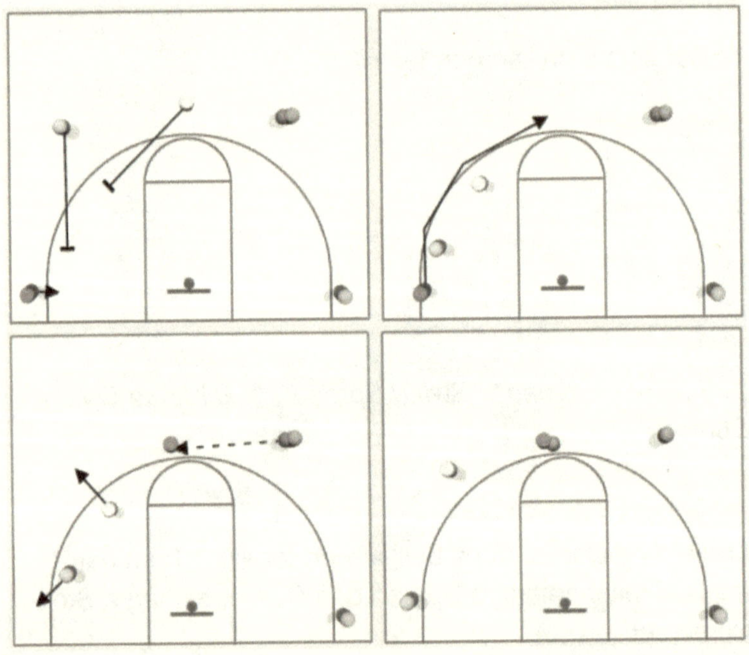

Examples: "Stagger", "Swing Stagger", "Exchange Swing Stagger-Pop Pin-Down-Pop"

Pin-down

This one assumes the ball has been centered and Trailer has it at the top of the key

Wing screens down for Corner. "Pin-Down Weak" - Weak-Side Wing screens down for Weak-Side Corner

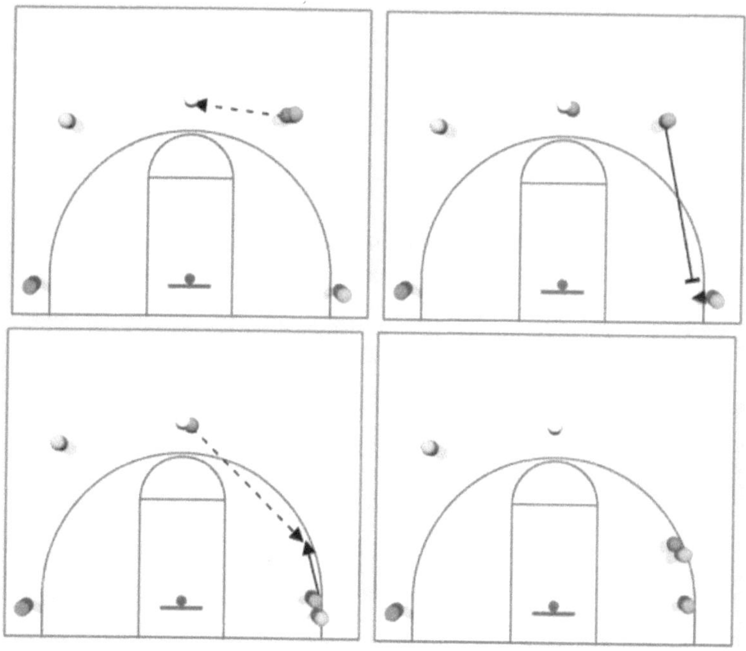

Examples: "Center Pin-Down", "Exchange Center Pin-Down", "Center Pin-Down Step-Up"

Away

Trailer screens for Weak-Side Wing. If Weak-Side Wing curls, Trailer pops back and is available for a pass and handoff with the Wing. If Weak-Side Wing pops, Trailer can turn and re-screen for Weak-Side Wing at the top of the key

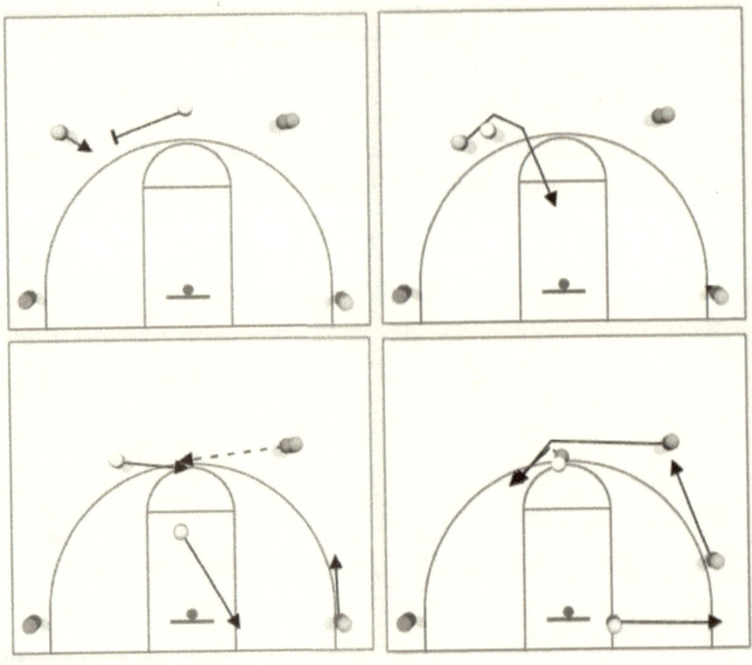

Examples: "Away", "Swing Away", "Exchange Away-Pop"

Flare

This one assumes the ball has been centered and Trailer has it at the top of the key

Corner lifts and sets a back-screen for Wing. "Flare Weak" - Weak-Side Corner sets a back-screen for Weak-Side Wing

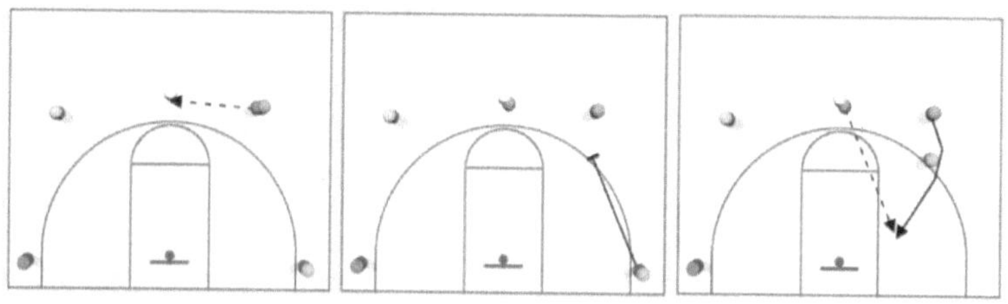

Examples: "Center Flare", "Center Flare-Weak", "Lift Corner Flare"

Flex

This one assumes Corner has pushed to the opposite block

Corner sets a screen for Weak-Side Corner on the block. Weak-Side Corner cuts all the way through to the opposite corner if they don't get the ball

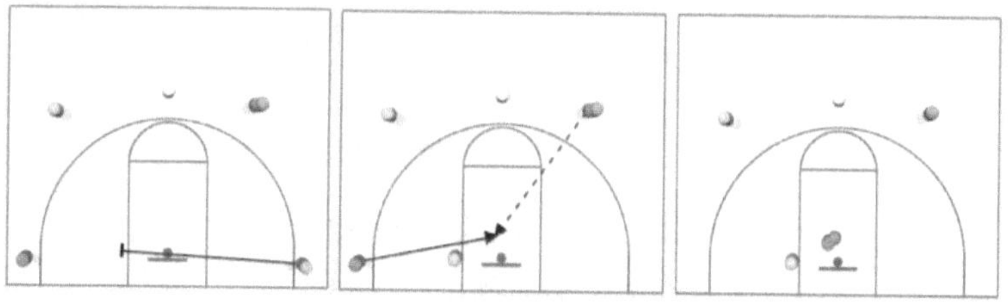

Examples: "Push Flex", "Exchange Push Flex", "Swing Push Flex"

Other

Pistol

This one assumes the ball has been centered and Trailer has it at the top of the key

Wing sets a Pin-Down screen for Corner and Trailer follows immediately behind with a Dribble-Handoff for Corner

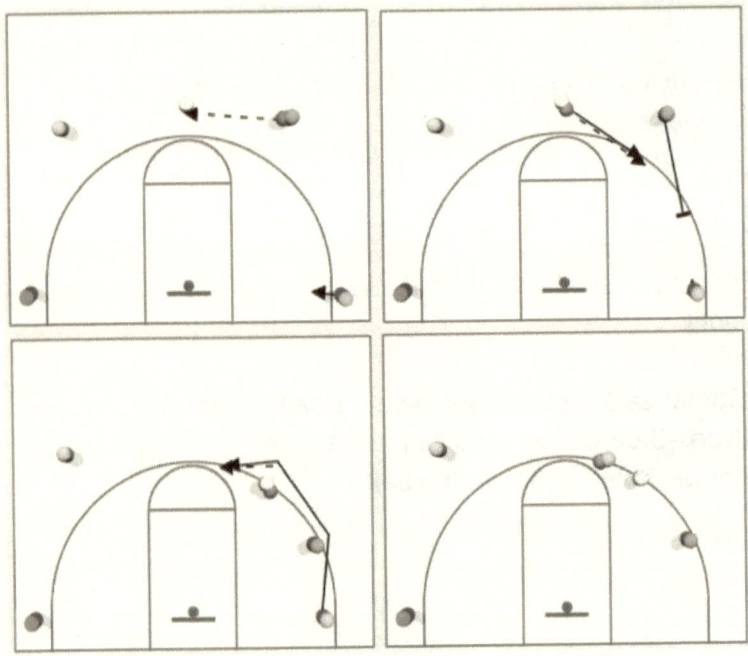

Examples: "Center Pistol", "Exchange Center Pistol-Weak", "Swing Stagger-Pop Pistol-Weak"

Dribble-at

This one assumes the ball has been centered and the Trailer has it at the top of the key

Trailer dribbles at Wing who can cut backdoor or go over the top and receive the dribble handoff. We don't call it a dribble handoff because we want to leave the options open for Wing to not receive a handoff

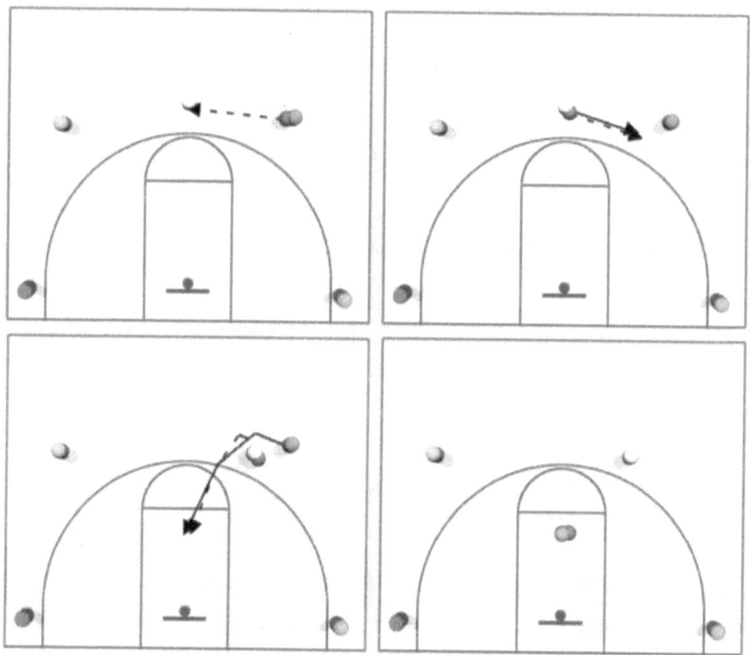

Examples: "Center Dribble-At", "Exchange Center Dribble-At-Weak"

Weak

The "weak" side of the floor is defined as the side of the floor opposite the ball. When the ball is in the middle of the floor, the "weak" side is opposite the side the ball was last on

For example, look at "Center Pin-Down-Weak" here

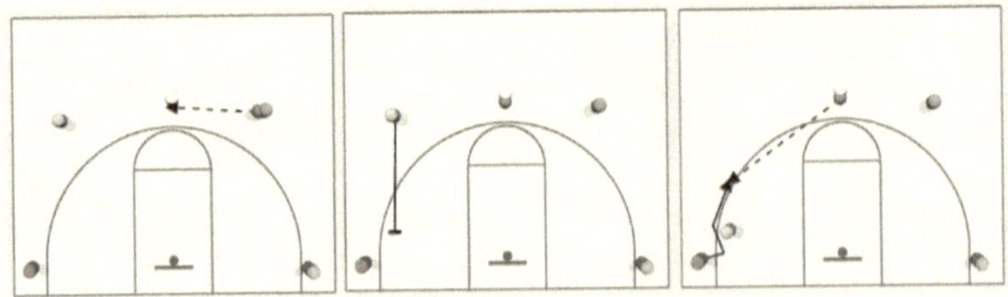

Compared with "Center Pin-Down"

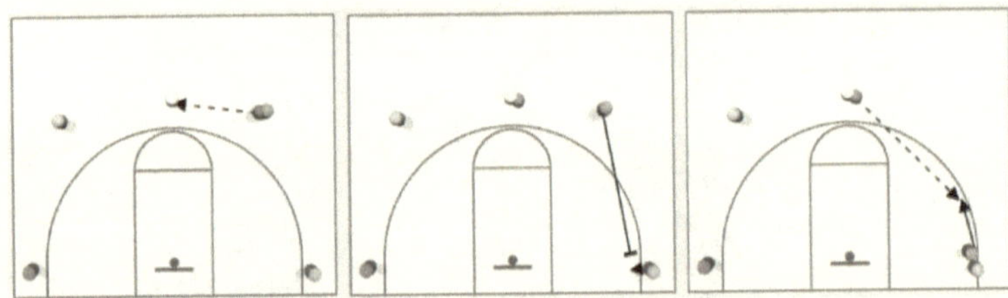

We know the weak-side of the floor because the ball never changed sides, so the weak-side stays the same until the ball changes sides

Reads

The below actions are sometimes called, but should be thought of more as reads and used to help communicate what to look for when coming off other actions

Pop, Curl, Reject, Fade

When coming off any screen, a player can pop, curl, Reject or fade

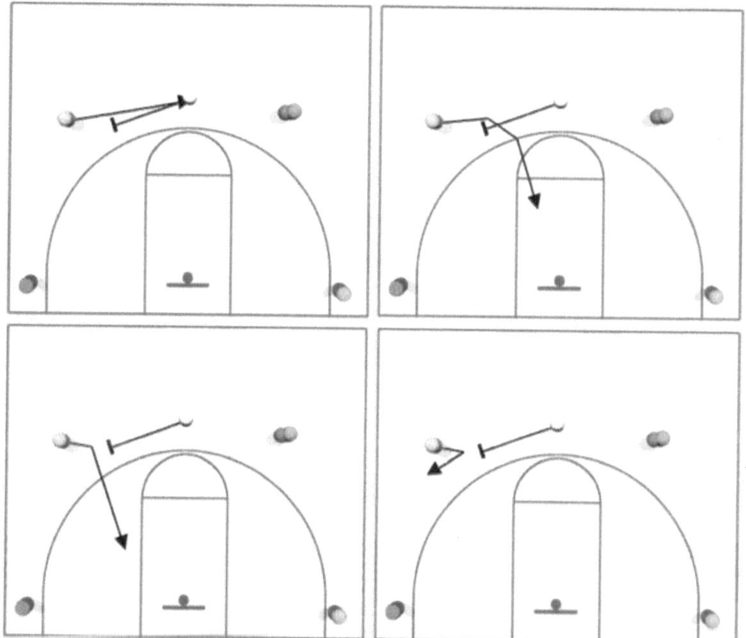

- *Pop* - the player receiving the screen comes straight off. Sometimes this will be a few steps beyond the screen, but can also be stopping behind the screen

- *Curl* - the player receiving the screen comes around tight off the screen towards the basket. This is normally done when a defender is playing very tightly but trailing behind the player receiving the screen

- *Reject* - the player receiving the screen doesn't use the screen, but sets the player up to think they are and then cuts it off normally towards the basket. This is normally done when a defender is being very aggressive to beat the offensive player through the screen

- *Fade* - the player receiving the screen starts to use the screen, but then fades back or out. This is normally done

when a defender runs under a screen and fading will
create space for a catch and shoot or drive opportunity

Slip

When setting a screen, a player can slip (normally to the
basket) before planting to set a screen

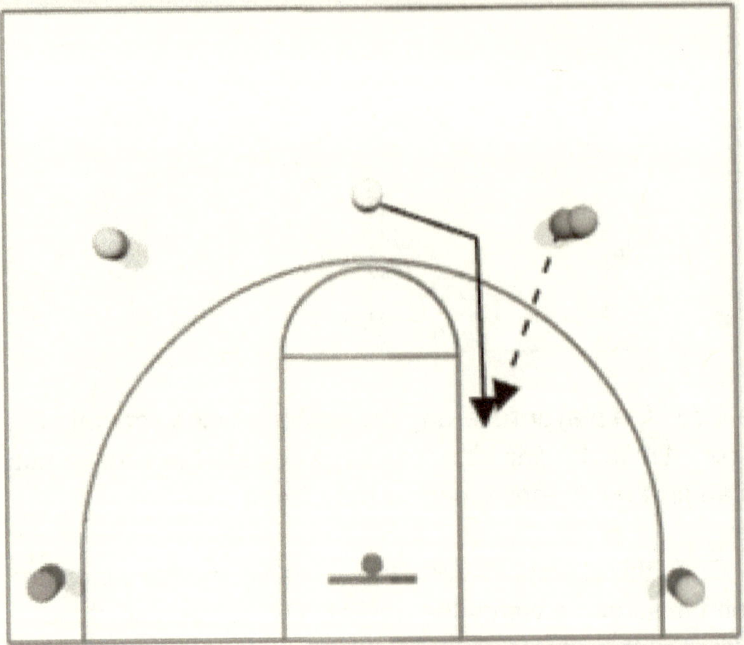

Reshape

When setting a screen, a player can reshape to set the
angle of the screen in the opposite direction of what would
be considered normal

ABO In Games

Now you know how to teach ABO and have a good list of actions to move your players around the floor like they are chess pieces - "we're playing chess not checkers" right? So - let's think about in-game strategy

Strategy

As I mentioned in the introduction, a big advantage of Action Based Offense is being able to make calls specifically for your personnel and sometimes more importantly, the personnel of the team you are playing

Since there are so many possibilities of strategic situations you could find yourself in, I will cover a few specific ones that will hopefully drive home the bigger concepts

Example 1 - Picking on the Defense

We played a team who had 4 quick guards who were solid defenders, but they had 1 big who didn't couldn't move

The big was guarding our trailer, so to take advantage of the big not wanting to come out, we decided to call a lot of Spread ball screens and we were able to get to the rim and draw fouls on the big

When the big got in foul trouble, they switched them to guard our weak-side corner - trying to get the big as far away from the ball as possible. To keep the big involved in defense, we started calling "Swing Step-Up" putting the big back in ball screen defense

No matter who they switched the big onto, we were able to get the ball there and force the big to play defense. We did this successfully in 2 games against them and were able to limit the minutes of the big due to foul trouble

Example 2 - Exposing Lack of Strategy

In another game, we played a team that had 5 solid defenders who you could tell were just told to go out and get stops. There was no communication on defense - no scheming to switch certain things or go over or under screens

We decided the best thing to do was hit them with a lot of variation so they couldn't figure things out in-game. We ran a different action combination every possession the first quarter and they couldn't stop it

It wasn't because we were doing anything fancy - it was because they were getting hit with a screen from a different direction at a different position on the floor every time down, so there was no figuring out what was coming next for them

These were our calls the first 10 times down the floor
- Spread
- Swing Away
- Center Pin-down
- Exchange Swing Stagger
- Center Flare
- Double
- Stagger
- Exchange Pistol
- Away
- Swing Spread

As a defense, if you aren't prepared for how you are going to guard ball screens or off-ball screens, this is an absolute nightmare because you have no idea what's coming and it's hard to find the pattern quickly in-game

Example 3 - Getting the Ball in Your Playmakers' Hands

We all get late in a game and know we want to feed our playmakers. ABO is great in this regard because you can get the ball in a specific player's hands every different way

Let's say you have a wing who you need to get the ball, but it's not as easy as calling ISO and getting a bucket.

You have to work a little to get the ball into an operating area and also move your playmaker around the floor, so it's not so obvious you are just trying to get them the ball

Think through this list of actions - all of which get the ball back in the starting wing's hands
- Spread
- Swing Away
- Exchange Center Pistol
- Center Swap Weak Double
- Center Dribble-at
- Exchange Swing Stagger
- Lift Corner Scissors Center Pistol Weak

There are 7 ways right there where we can get the ball in one player's hands in a different spot or coming off a different type of screen. That's almost an entire quarter's worth of different "play calls" and the list and combination of actions can go on-and-on

Calling ABO

So you might be thinking "well, that sounds good, but it's not going to sound good when I'm on the sideline yelling *'Exchange Swing Stagger-Pop Pin-Down-Pop'*" and I hear you

At first, calling the actions is going to feel awkward, but calling them explicitly is a great way to learn and it's easy to communicate

Eventually, you will get to a point where you find a few combinations that work really well either in getting players where you want them or helping you break down a defense

This is when you can start combining actions into sets

> *Note the difference between "set" and "play" and what that communicates. "Set" indicates that this is a starting point - it isn't a script that must be followed and continued*

For example, we had sets *One, Two, Three* and *Four*

- *One* - Swing Stagger-Pop Pin-Down
- *Two* - Exchange Center
- *Three* - Center Swap Weak
- *Four* - Lift Corner Scissors Center

We could then call "One Step-Up" or "Four Dribble-At" and we are running 2 to 4 actions and then able to have another action after that. The number of possible combinations here is literally growing exponentially with no additional knowledge required of your players

Further Considerations

In this book, we've only talked about ABO from a 5-Out set. Some new positioning and terminology would have to change, but I think another great starting set would be a Horns set or a 4-Around-1 set

I think with more advanced teams and after implementing in a program for a couple years, it would be very likely to call "Horns Pin-Down" or "5 (5-Out) Pin-Down" giving another layer of variation

I've never played or coached at the professional level, but when putting this in and thinking through the system, I reached out to some coaches I know at the NBA level and learned that this type of "play-calling" is very similar to what they do. For example, one NBA call was "dribble roll" which is a dribble handoff to a pick and roll - ABO gives a well defined structure for making these calls and communicating them to your team

I would love to hear any feedback or suggestions on these concepts as they are still somewhat new to me and something I've just started implementing in my very young coaching career

As I was completing this book, I ran across some really good resources that expand on the idea of creating and improving on an offensive advantage - I encourage you to check those out
- SABA: The Antifragile Offense by Brian McCormick
- BasketballImmersion.com - BDT and Zero Decision Basketball

More Resources

The illustrations in this book are created with a tool that I built and can be found at https://stevenkaspar.com/playmaker. If you would like the playbook of actions I used to load into the tool for the pictures, send me an email at me@stevenkaspar.com with the subject "Action Based Offense Playbook Please" and I will get that to you. It is a free tool for anyone

You can get in touch by email at me@stevenkaspar.com or on Instagram or LinkedIn or wherever else I have a social media account - I'd love to hear from you

Please, leave a review with what you thought of the book and check out my other work!